IT'S MY STATE!

MINNESOTA

Marlene Targ Brill

Elizabeth Kaplan

mc **Marshall Cavendish**
Benchmark
New York

Website: www.marshallcavendish.us

This publication represents the opinions and views of the authors based on their personal experience, knowledge, and research. The information in this book serves as a general guide only. The authors and publisher have used their best efforts in preparing this book and disclaim liability rising directly and indirectly from the use and application of this book.

Other Marshall Cavendish Offices:
Marshall Cavendish International (Asia) Private Limited, 1 New Industrial Road, Singapore 536196 •
Marshall Cavendish International (Thailand) Co Ltd. 253 Asoke, 12th Flr, Sukhumvit 21 Road, Klongtoey Nua, Wattana, Bangkok 10110, Thailand • Marshall Cavendish (Malaysia) Sdn Bhd, Times Subang, Lot 46, Subang Hi-Tech Industrial Park, Batu Tiga, 40000 Shah Alam, Selangor Darul Ehsan, Malaysia

Marshall Cavendish is a trademark of Times Publishing Limited

All websites were available and accurate when this book was sent to press.

Library of Congress Cataloging-in-Publication Data
Brill, Marlene Targ.
        Minnesota / Marlene Targ Brill and Elizabeth Kaplan. — 2nd ed.
           p. cm. — (It's my state!)
        Includes index.
        ISBN 978-1-60870-054-7
        1. Minnesota—Juvenile literature. I. Kaplan, Elizabeth, 1956- II. Title.
    F606.3.B75 2011
    977.6—dc22   2010003909

Second Edition developed for Marshall Cavendish Benchmark by RJF Publishing LLC (www.RJFpublishing.com)
Series Designer, Second Edition: Tammy West/Westgraphix LLC
Editor, Second Edition: William A. McGeveran

All maps, illustrations, and graphics © Marshall Cavendish Corporation. Maps and artwork on pages 6, 28, 29, 75, 76, and back cover by Christopher Santoro. Map and graphics on pages 8 and 45 by Westgraphix LLC.

The photographs in this book are used by permission and through the courtesy of:
Front cover: Judy Flower and Jacek Chabraszewski (inset)/Shutterstock (both).
Alamy: © Clint Farlinger, 4 (top), 13; © America, 10; © Marvin Dembinsky Photo Associates, 11; © Scott Kemper, 12; © Alaska Stock LLC, 15; © Reimar, 19; © Lyroky, 24; © North Wind Picture Archives, 27 (both), 35; © Steve Skjold, 42, 46 (bottom), 50, 53; © CLEO Photo, 44; © GREG RYAN, 46 (top), 52, 57; © Nathan Benn, 47; © Gail Mooney-Kelly, 60; © EdBockStock, 62; Richard Levine, 66; © Andre Jenny, 69; © Keith Levit Photography, 74. **AP Images:** Eric Miller, 49 (top). **Getty Images:** 73; Tom Walker, 4 (bottom); Still Images, 5; Annie Griffiths Belt/National Geographic, 17, 20; Joe McDonald/Visuals Unlimited, 18 (top); Stephen J. Krasemann, 18 (bottom); Sylvia Duran Sharnoff/National Geographic, 21 (top); Ken Lucas/National Geographic, 21 (bottom); David Boyer/National Geographic, 22; SSPL; Hulton Archive, 26; Mark Wilson, 40; Bachrach/Hulton Archive, 48; Simon Bruty/Sports Illustrated, 49 (bottom); Mark Brettingen/National Football League, 59; Hulton Archive, 61; Tom Grill, 64, 70; Ken Lucas/Visuals Unlimited, 67; Bill Alkofer, 68; Jeff Sherman, 71 (top); Wally Eberhart, 71 (bottom); Mark Erickson, 72. **iStockphoto:** © Lawrence Sawyer, 51. **Minnesota Historical Society:** 25, 36, 39; Edward K. Thomas, 30; Joel Emmons Whitney, 31; Frederic Remington, 33; Harry D. Ayer, 34. **Shutterstock:** John McLaird, 9; Geoffrey Kuchera, 54. **Paul Stafford:** 14.

Printed in Malaysia (T).
135642

CONTENTS

State Tree: Norway Pine

Most of the Norway pines in Minnesota are found in the northern and northeastern parts of the state. As the tree ages, the bark begins to turn reddish, which is why this tree is also known as the red pine. Minnesota's tallest red pine is 120 feet (37 meters) tall and over three hundred years old.

State Bird: Common Loon

This black-and-white bird can be seen gliding gently across Minnesota lakes. One of the world's oldest surviving bird species, loons can dive more than 100 feet (30 m) underwater in search of food and can stay underwater for nearly five minutes. Minnesota has more loons than any other state except Alaska.

State Flower: Pink and White Lady Slipper

Lady slippers dot Minnesota's wetlands, bogs, and forests with their beautiful pink-and-white bowl-like flowers. The plants grow slowly, taking four to sixteen years to flower. They may live for up to a hundred years and grow 4 feet (1.2 m) tall. It is illegal to pick this flower without permission from the state.

State Muffin: Blueberry

In 1988, a group of third-grade children in the town of Carlton convinced the state legislature to make the blueberry muffin the state muffin. The children noted that the main ingredients in the muffins—blueberries and wheat—were both important to the state. Wild blueberries grow in the swamps, forests, and hills of northeastern Minnesota. Farmers all around the state grow wheat.

State Gemstone: Lake Superior Agate

Lake Superior agate is found in rocks that formed billions of years ago. This mineral is known for the beautiful lines of red, yellow, and orange that form designs in it. The lines are thin bands of iron. Pieces of agate are often polished and used in jewelry.

State Drink: Milk

Minnesota cows produce around 9 billion pounds (4 billion kilograms) of milk each year. The state generally ranks fifth or sixth in the nation for milk production. So it makes sense that Minnesotans chose milk as their state drink.

The Land of 10,000 Lakes

Minnesota has sky-blue waters, blankets of forest, and acres of sweeping fertile flatland. The state's different terrains, plus a wide range of weather from north to south, make Minnesota seem like several states in one. It is the fourteenth largest state, with a land area of 79,610 square miles (206,189 square kilometers).

The name *Minnesota* comes from a Dakota word meaning "water that reflects the sky." Known as the "Land of 10,000 Lakes," Minnesota really has more than 20,000 lakes. Almost 12,000 of them are at least 10 acres (4 hectares) in area.

Where did all the lakes and rivers come from? Scientists say that about 11,000 to 12,000 years ago, most of Minnesota was covered by glaciers—huge sheets of slow-moving ice. As the glaciers moved in, they flattened hills and dug out valleys. As they moved out, they deposited soil, sand, and rocks and left behind many holes filled with ice. Lakes formed when the ice melted. Rivers formed as the melting ice drained away.

Minnesota can be divided into four geographic regions, based on the main ecosystem in each region. Mixed forests of evergreen and deciduous trees (those

Quick Facts

MINNESOTA BORDERS

North	Canada
South	Iowa
East	Wisconsin
	Lake Superior
West	North Dakota
	South Dakota

Minnesota Counties

Minnesota has 87 counties.

Woods and clouds are reflected on the surface of this beautiful lake in the mixed-forest region of northern Minnesota.

that lose their leaves in the fall) cover northeastern and north-central Minnesota. Deciduous forests extend in a diagonal band from the northwest down to the southeast, where they occupy that corner of the state. Tallgrass prairies cover most of the state's west. A small region in the northwest has a mix of tallgrass prairie and aspen woods.

Mixed Forests

Mixed forests, with pine, aspen, and birch trees, blanket northeastern Minnesota. This area is shaped like an arrowhead, with Canada to the north and Lake Superior to the south and east. It is the snowiest part of the state. Minnesota's tallest peak, Eagle Mountain, is located here. It rises 2,301 feet (701 m) above sea level. Lake Superior makes up 150 miles (240 kilometers) of the area's varied shoreline. Boaters on the beautiful lake can see waterfalls tumbling down cliffs some 1,000 feet

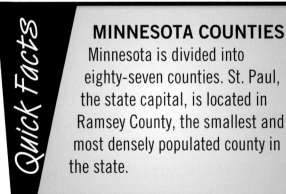

Quick Facts

MINNESOTA COUNTIES
Minnesota is divided into eighty-seven counties. St. Paul, the state capital, is located in Ramsey County, the smallest and most densely populated county in the state.

(300 m) high. Through the port of Duluth on Lake Superior, Minnesota is connected to the other four Great Lakes, to the St. Lawrence River, and finally to the Atlantic Ocean.

The Arrowhead area is famous for its Boundary Waters Canoe Area Wilderness, which straddles the border with Canada. Here, more than a thousand lakes and streams cut through lush forests. People can travel for hours in nonmotorized boats, stopping to fish or simply to enjoy the area's peaceful beauty.

Northern Minnesota includes the northernmost point in the United States outside Alaska. This "point" is actually within a huge lake called Lake of the Woods. The town of Angle Inlet is located on a section of Minnesota land that juts into Lake of the Woods. It is the northernmost town in the lower forty-eight states.

The region also includes the Mesabi Range, where rocky hills zigzag 130 miles (210 km) from south of Ely to Grand Rapids. The range gets its name from an Ojibwe legend about a red giant named Mesabe who slept in the earth. In 1887, a miner discovered iron ore in the range, and Minnesota soon became one of America's key iron-mining states.

North-central Minnesota also has mixed forests of evergreen and deciduous trees. In addition, this area has many lakes and large areas of wetlands. The source of the Mississippi River is located in this region. People come long distances to Minnesota's oldest state park, Itasca State Park, to walk across the mighty river at its source. From there, the Mississippi travels south about 2,340 miles (3,765 km) to reach the Gulf of Mexico. Starting as a trickle, the waters of the Mississippi grow into the largest river in North America in terms of volume of water carried.

Deciduous Forests

In the southeast and a band extending diagonally across the rest of the state is a region of deciduous forests that include maple, ash, oak, and elm trees. The region has open woods and scattered prairies. The Saint Croix, Minnesota,

The scenic Saint Croix, one of the state's major rivers, flows along the Minnesota-Wisconsin border before finally emptying into the Mississippi.

Maples, birches, and other deciduous trees show off their fall colors as they spread over rolling hills in the southeastern part of the state.

and other large rivers have cut deep valleys through the landscape. They give Minnesota some of its most dramatic scenery.

The southeastern corner of Minnesota has rolling, forest-covered hills cut by deep streams that rush down to join the Mississippi River. Drier hillsides are covered with waving grasses. The last set of glaciers from the north did not scrape across this area of Minnesota. That is why it is much more rugged than the rest of the state.

Western Prairies

Western Minnesota is generally drier than eastern parts of the state. For this reason, prairies (grasslands) rather than forests are the main ecosystem. About ten thousand years ago, this area was at the bottom of part of a huge lake called Lake Agassiz, which formed as the glaciers melted. After the lake drained away a few thousand years later, the deepest part of the lake became a flat, fertile plain. Today, the Red River flows across this region. The Red River Valley is known for its oats, corn, and bright yellow sunflowers.

Tallgrass prairie once covered huge areas of Minnesota and the whole Midwest. Hundreds of plant and animal species are preserved in the portions of it that remain today.

Like a typical Minnesota kid, this boy is happy to brave frigid temperatures in order to have fun in the snow.

Aspen Woods and Prairies

The aspen woods and prairies in part of northern Minnesota make up the smallest of the state's natural regions. This region forms a transition between the mixed forests to the east and the tallgrass prairies to the west. The area also was once covered by Lake Agassiz. However, the lake was shallower here than it was to the west, and the lake bottom was made up mainly of sand or rocks. So the soil today is less fertile, and less of the prairie has been converted to farmland.

The Climate

Minnesotans joke that their state's climate is "ten months of winter and two months of rough sledding." Snow covers much of the state from mid-December to mid-March. The snowiest part of Minnesota, along Lake Superior, gets close to 6 feet (almost 2 m) of snow every winter. Even the drier southwestern region averages 3 feet (almost 1 m) of snow yearly. And with Minnesota's cold winters, the snow sticks around. In Minneapolis, which is in the southern part of the state, January temperatures average 13 degrees Fahrenheit (–10.6 degrees Celsius), and the average winter has thirty days when the temperature falls to 0 °F (–18 °C) or lower. Places in northern Minnesota have from time to time reported

Quick Facts

HOW COLD CAN IT GET?
The coldest temperature ever to be recorded in Minnesota was –60 °F (–51 °C), which was reached near the town of Tower on February 2, 1996.

winter temperatures close to –40 °F (–40 °C). There is no question about it: Minnesotans need plenty of warm clothes because the state gets very cold and snowy in the winter.

In Minnesota's larger cities, people use skyways—enclosed, aboveground walkways between buildings—to avoid the cold. At night, some Minnesotans plug their cars into electric warmers to keep the engines from freezing. But for those who love winter sports, Minnesota is a paradise. Snow-covered hills are great for sledding and downhill skiing. Forest paths are used for cross-country skiing and snowmobiling. Frozen lakes provide places to skate and play hockey. When the ice gets thick enough, many Minnesotans walk out on the surface and go fishing. They cut holes in the ice to drop in fishing lines. When the ice gets really thick, some people even drive onto the lake and set up an ice-fishing shack—a hut or other shelter to block the wind. They can often leave the shelter up for much of the winter.

Summer may come as a relief to many Minnesotans, but it is not always a reward. Normal July temperatures in

In Their Own Words

You know you are a true Minnesotan when you have more miles on your snow blower than on your car.

—Typical joke about the weather

Two girls, joined by a golden retriever, enjoy cross-country skiing on a winter's day in Minnesota.

GLOBAL WARMING IN MINNESOTA?
Over the past century, Minnesota's climate actually got slightly warmer, by an average of about 1 °F (0.56 °C). Many scientists believe that this warming could speed up in the rest of the present century and that an increase in so-called greenhouse gases in the atmosphere is a major cause. While not a few Minnesotans might welcome warmer weather, climate change (which scientists think is happening globally) could harm the state's forests, water resources, and plants and animals. The state has a plan to reduce the amount of greenhouse gases added to the atmosphere, partly by increasing the use of renewable energy resources. Most of the greenhouse gases added to the atmosphere are a result of burning fuels such as heating oil, gasoline, and coal.

Minneapolis range from about 63 °F to 83 °F (17 °C to 28 °C), but it can get hotter than that. The temperature in Minneapolis has gone as high as 105 °F (40.5 °C). In Moorhead on July 6, 1936, the temperature reached a record high for the state, hitting 114 °F (46 °C). Minnesotans who prefer cooler weather can head to the shores of Lake Superior during the summer. The surface of the massive lake acts like a giant air conditioner, cooling the air above it, which then blows onshore and cools shore areas to comfortable levels.

Wildlife

Minnesota's different ecosystems allow for a wide variety of plants and animals. Bluestem grasses, blazingstar flowers, black-eyed Susans, and prairie smoke flowers are among the many colorful plants that brighten the prairie. Trees add year-round interest. Aspen trees are common in the deciduous and mixed forests. In summer, their leaves shimmer in the breeze. Maple trees grow in many parts of the state. In the fall, their leaves turn beautiful shades of orange, red, and yellow. Pine, spruce, and other evergreen trees dominate parts of northern and eastern Minnesota. In the winter, they add dark beauty to the snow-covered Minnesota landscape.

Sugar maples are a common sight, turning an array of striking colors in the fall.

The fields and forests are also home to deer, beavers, raccoons, and squirrels. In the woods, you may see skunks, martens, porcupines, and red and gray foxes. The howls of wolves and coyote often pierce the night. Larger animals include moose, elk, and black bears.

Minnesota has a large bird population. Common songbirds such as robins, cardinals, goldfinches, and many others nest in the state. Water-loving species, including Canada geese, mallards, and wood ducks, also abound. In addition, the state lies at the northern edge of the Mississippi flyway, a long migration route taken by birds as they travel to and from their winter homes farther south. About a hundred species of birds migrate through Minnesota every year. There may be hundreds of thousands of birds flying through at any given time.

However, some birds that had been very common in Minnesota have begun to drop in numbers. For example, eastern meadowlarks, red-headed woodpeckers, and northern pintail ducks all are on the decline. Scientists think these birds have fewer good places to find food and to nest because more people now settle or vacation on grasslands, in woods, and along waterways. Minnesotans are

Quick Facts

MARTEN UPS AND DOWNS

Martens are weasel-like animals that live in forests. Because of their valuable fur, they were hunted almost to extinction in Minnesota by the early 1900s. However, the marten population has rebounded. Today, there are more than ten thousand martens in northern Minnesota, enough to support the trapping of a few thousand a year. It is said that the number of martens now trapped each year may be higher than it was in the early fur-trading days.

working to keep wild lands wild. They also plant native species of flowers, trees, and shrubs in their yards and parks to help attract birds.

Aquatic, or water-loving, animals thrive in Minnesota. Several types of salamanders, frogs, snakes, and turtles live in and around the state's waterways.

Minnesota's waters are home to many fish species, and the state has a big sports fishing industry. Minnesota sells more fishing licenses for the size of its population than any other state. Among the most popular fish are walleye, northern pike, bass, and muskie.

Beavers thrive along the state's woodland streams.

Canada geese are among the many water-loving birds that make their home in the state.

Preservation and Protection

Federal, state, and local governments work together with residents to preserve and protect Minnesota's wildlife. Hunting is limited by state regulation. Laws have been passed to prevent people from killing protected animals or disturbing the habitats of animals that are threatened or endangered. Minnesota's plant life is also protected. It is illegal to pick any plants that the government has listed as endangered or threatened.

Minnesotans have also worked on their own to help preserve the state's natural environment. An example is the Minnesota Conservation Corps (MCC), which was started by the state legislature in 1981 and now operates without state funding. Through this organization, young people take on jobs involving such tasks as building trails and log shelters, improving campgrounds, and keeping track of how well different kinds of animals are surviving in the wild.

In Their Own Words

Every river swarms, every bay is a reservoir [storage lake] of magnificent fish.

—Robert Roosevelt (President Theodore Roosevelt's uncle), talking about fishing in Minnesota

Gray Wolf

Despite their name, not all gray wolves are gray. Some have tan, reddish, brown, or black fur. Gray wolves usually hunt in packs of six to twelve. Once nearly extinct in the United States outside Alaska, they grew in numbers after being protected. Today, there are a few thousand gray wolves in Minnesota. They are now listed by the state as threatened—that is, at risk of becoming endangered and thus possibly extinct.

Monarch Butterfly

Minnesota is home to more than a hundred different species, or types, of butterflies. Unlike many species, the state's monarch butterflies travel to a warmer place for the winter. After spending the summer in Minnesota, they fly south all the way to central Mexico. Their journey takes several months and covers some 1,800 miles (3,000 km).

Moose

Moose can weigh more than 1,000 pounds (450 kg). Their long legs and the shape of their hooves help them move easily in marshy areas and along lakes and streams, where they browse. They can even dive to the bottom of shallow lakes to rip apart plant life there. There are now about five thousand to eight thousand moose in the state. Their numbers have been falling greatly in northwestern Minnesota; many scientists believe warmer weather is partly to blame.

Morel Mushroom

These brown, spongy-topped mushrooms add an unusual flavor to many foods. Each spring, expert mushroom hunters search Minnesota's fields and forests for morels. But they have to watch out, because mushrooms that look a lot like morels may be poisonous. Eating the wrong mushroom can cause severe illness, and even death.

Wild Rice

Wild rice can be found in shallow bodies of water mainly in northern and central Minnesota. It has been gathered throughout Minnesota's history and at one time was found throughout the state. American Indians who lived in the area many hundreds of years ago harvested and ate the rice. Minnesotans still harvest wild rice today.

Walleye

Big, marblelike eyes with white pupils give this fish its name—and its excellent vision, which is useful for hunting prey. The walleye is important to the state's huge sportsfishing industry. Most walleyes caught and kept in Minnesota weigh just over a pound (0.5 kg). But the largest walleye caught in the state weighed more than 17 pounds, 8 ounces (almost 8 kg).

From the Beginning

Thousands of years ago, migrants crossed from Asia into North America. Some traveled across a northern land bridge that once connected Siberia and Alaska. In time, these early peoples spread throughout North America, eventually reaching the region that is now Minnesota.

Early Minnesotans

Before the arrival of Europeans, generation after generation of American Indians in the region gathered plants, fished, and hunted wild animals for food and clothing. They learned to carve stone and bone and later to shape copper into tools. To honor their dead, later groups started burying them in huge mounds made of earth. Some of these mounds are still visible today. One of the largest is Grand Mound, near International Falls. It is 100 feet (30 m) long and 45 feet (14 m) tall. It serves as a reminder of the people who lived in Minnesota long ago.

By 1000 BCE the land had features similar to those of today. Forests dominated the northern and eastern parts of Minnesota and prairies were established in the west. Native peoples in the prairies developed a lifestyle centered on hunting deer and bison (commonly called buffalo). Groups that spent more time in and around forests and lakes developed a lifestyle based on fishing.

Over time, these different lifestyles became more complex. Groups that hunted on the prairies started to harvest wild rice. They found ways to store the

An Ojibwe girl looks at rock carvings made thousands of years before her own ancestors settled in the region.

In a diorama at the Pipestone National Monument, in southwest Minnesota, Indians of the past are shown mining red stone from that site. Continuing a long cultural tradition, Minnesota Indians use this red stone today to create handmade pipes in many styles and designs.

rice by roasting it, so as to have more food to eat in the winter months. Groups that spent more time in and around the forests planted squash seeds in the fertile soil of the river valleys. They also began raising corn and beans, which could be prepared for winter storage. These changes helped both groups flourish.

Agriculture based on corn and beans became very important to Indians living in what is now southern Minnesota. They built large, permanent villages near their gardens. They also went on trips north to hunt, fish, and gather wild foods.

By the time the first Europeans arrived in North America, Indians in what is now Minnesota had been following the same cultural patterns for centuries. There were several major groups. The Ioway, who were closely related to the Winnebago in Wisconsin, lived in the river valleys of the southeast. The Dakota lived where the prairies and forests came together in north-central Minnesota. The Europeans called these Indians Sioux—which means "snake" and implies "enemy." The Dakota were related to the Assiniboine, who lived in northwestern Minnesota. Another group, the Cheyenne, lived just north of the Dakota, along the Upper Mississippi River.

The Europeans soon started trading with Indian tribes. The Indians provided animal furs, which were very popular in Europe for coats and hats, in exchange for strong, durable tools, pots, and weapons made of iron. This trade was profitable for both groups. But it led to fierce competition among Indian tribes as well as among the European nations.

By the time the first Europeans set foot in what is now Minnesota, around 1660, many tribes in the East were pushing westward into the area. One of their main goals was to expand their fur-hunting grounds. They came into conflict with the Indians already living there. As the fur trade grew, more tribes became involved, and conflicts intensified. By the 1680s, the Ioway had been pushed out of what is now Minnesota. The Dakota were under pressure from the Ojibwe, who had come into the region from the area north and east of Lake Superior.

The Ojibwe, whose name was mispronounced "Chippewa" by French traders, had a lifestyle fairly similar to that of the Dakota. One difference was their beautiful, light birchbark canoes. The Dakota, in contrast, made their canoes from hollowed-out logs. In winter, when the lakes and rivers were frozen, the Ojibwe used snowshoes to travel quickly over the land.

The Dakota and the Ojibwe had shared hunting grounds for decades, but competition over the fur trade made them bitter enemies. As the Ojibwe settled

This picture, by the artist Frederic Remington, depicts a friendly handshake between a fur trader and an Indian leader. The fur trade benefited both sides but led to bitter competition among Indian tribes.

Members of the Ojibwe tribe are shown building lodges from a framework of wooden poles.

onto Dakota lands, the Dakota were gradually forced out of the northern half of what is now Minnesota.

French Explorers Arrive

The French set up fur-trading posts in eastern Canada in the early 1600s and explored many parts of North America. The first Europeans to explore the area that is now Minnesota were the French fur traders Pierre Radisson and Médard Chouart, whose title was sieur des Groseilliers. In 1660, Radisson and Groseilliers traveled through this region in search of the Northwest Passage—a water route linking the Atlantic and Pacific oceans. They did not find it (it was not there to be found). What they found instead were deep forests and abundant waterways.

In 1679, Daniel Greysolon, sieur Du Lhut (also spelled Duluth), began a long journey through the area on behalf of France. He worked to make peace among warring Indian tribes, hoping this would benefit the French fur trade. Du Lhut helped strengthen French control over the area that is now Minnesota. Years later, the city of Duluth was named after him. Another well-known figure was the French explorer and missionary Father Louis Hennepin. One of the state's counties is named after him.

In the next century, French traders traveled throughout the region. They soon came into conflict with the British, who competed to build a fur-trading empire in North America. By 1754, the competition between Britain and France had erupted into the French and Indian War. This conflict, which also involved Indian tribes, ended in defeat for France in 1763. Under the treaty ending the war, Britain officially gained control of virtually all the land that France had claimed in North America east of the Mississippi River, including present-day eastern Minnesota. Eventually, most of the French moved from this area. But the French names of many places in Minnesota, including such towns as Elysian, Cloquet, and Belle Plaine, indicate the importance of the French in the region's history.

This French map of the Great Lakes region dates back to about 1700.

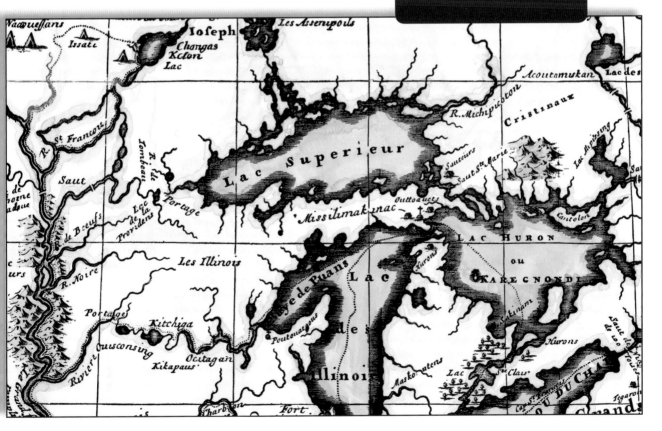

MAKING MODEL SNOWSHOES

Snowshoes let people walk on top of snow without sinking into it. When new settlers came to the region, they were impressed by the snowshoes the Ojibwe wore. The Ojibwe made their snowshoes out of animal hide and wood. You can make your model snowshoes out of pipe cleaners.

WHAT YOU NEED

Strong scissors

Seven brown or tan pipe cleaners, each 12 inches (30 cm) long

Two pieces of embroidery thread or very thin string, each about 4 to 5 feet (1.2 to 1.5 m) long

Cut one pipe cleaner in thirds. Cut one of the three pieces in half.

Lay two brown pipe cleaners side by side. Wrap one of the smallest pipe-cleaner pieces around the pair at one end. Repeat at the other end. This makes the frame. Spread out the frame so it is widest in the middle and is pointed at both ends. It will make a leaf shape. Attach each of the two middle-size pipe-cleaner pieces across the frame, somewhere between the middle and each end of the snowshoe. Wrap the ends of the pipe-cleaner pieces around the frame. These form the crosspieces.

Tie the end of one piece of embroidery thread to a crosspiece near the outside frame. Wrap it up and down around the two crosspieces over and over. When you have used nearly half of the thread, wrap it in the other direction, from side to side across the frame. Do not pull tight or you will change the shape of the frame. Tie the end of the thread to a crosspiece or to the frame.

Bend one tip of the snowshoe up. This is the front.

Cut about one-fourth of another pipe cleaner and loop it around several pieces of thread in the middle of the snowshoe. This would hold the person's foot onto the snowshoe.

Repeat the previous steps to create the other snowshoe. When you are finished, you can show your model snowshoes to your friends and family. You can also try to imagine what it must have been like for the Indians and early settlers who used snowshoes to walk through the Minnesota wilderness in the winter.

The Road to Statehood

In 1775, the American colonists began their successful war for independence from Great Britain. Under a peace treaty with Britain that officially ended the American Revolution in 1783, the new United States gained control of lands east of the Mississippi River, including present-day eastern Minnesota. Twenty years later, in 1803, the United States bought the Louisiana Territory from France. This action—known as the Louisiana Purchase—added to the United States a huge area west of the Mississippi River, including the rest of what became the state of Minnesota.

In the early 1800s, the United States purchased from the Dakota Indians an important parcel of land along the Mississippi River. It included Saint Anthony Falls and the strategic spot where the Minnesota River joins the Mississippi. The United States Army arrived at the spot in 1819 and, under the command of Colonel Josiah Snelling, built a fort there. The sturdy outpost was named Fort Saint Anthony, after the nearby waterfalls. After Snelling's death, the fort was renamed in his honor.

Fort Snelling was a remote outpost built by the U.S. Army in the early 1800s at a strategic spot near where the Minnesota River joins the Mississippi.

This photo shows Saint Anthony Falls, on the Mississippi, and the early settlement that grew into the modern city of Minneapolis.

The area had long been a trading spot for American Indians, many of them loyal to the British in Canada. After Fort Snelling was built, European-American settlers began arriving. Some were families of people involved in the fur trade. A group of refugees from a failed settlement in Canada were among the first permanent settlers of European heritage. The fort had the region's earliest post office, school, and hospital. It also had a flour mill and a lumber mill. In time, the settlements in the area grew into the cities of Minneapolis and St. Paul.

This growth was slow at first. The region was remote and was very cold and isolated in winter. There was no mail service or outside trade for close to half the year. But the area had many resources, including forests rich with timber. Much of the land was Indian territory, but the U.S. government continued to pressure the Dakota and Ojibwe to give up land. Treaties signed by the Ojibwe in 1851 required most of them to leave their forests in the upper half of the region. The Dakota sold all their land east of the Red River; in return, they received only a small strip of land along the Minnesota River.

With the Indians relocated, settlers felt safer moving to the region. Steamboat travel to the area increased. Many steamboats landed at a dock near Fort Snelling known as Pig's Eye Landing. In the early 1840s, a Roman Catholic missionary built a small church nearby, dedicated to St. Paul, and Pig's Eye Landing developed into a booming port settlement. It was named St. Paul, after the mission church.

Between 1853 and 1857, the region's population grew from 40,000 to 150,000 people. The area was large enough to be granted statehood. In 1858, Minnesota became the thirty-second state. St. Paul was chosen as the capital.

Growing Pains

The new state continued to grow into the 1860s. Small farms sprouted on the plains. Villages sprang up along waterways. The telegraph connected distant towns. The U.S. government offered money to build a network of railroads. To find workers, railroad companies arranged to have steamship lines bring European immigrants into Minnesota.

Around the same time, the U.S. government passed a law (known as the Homestead Act) granting 160 acres (65 hectares) of land in the American Midwest or Far West to anyone who agreed to build and live on the land for five years. Many immigrants came to Minnesota from western and northern Europe, especially Sweden, Norway, and Germany. They were eager to own land and start farms in the new state.

From 1861 to 1865, the Civil War raged between the Northern (Union) and

Quick Facts

HISTORY COMES ALIVE
The Minnesota Historical Society operates a History Center in St. Paul as well as more than two dozen other museums and historic sites around the state. They include Fort Snelling, the home of Minnesota's first governor, the mansion of railroad magnate James J. Hill, the 1860s farm of Oliver H. Kelley, a flour-mill museum, and an 1870's general store.

Southern (Confederate) states. Minnesota sent almost 24,000 soldiers to fight in Union armies. (The Union's victory in 1865 resulted in the end of slavery in the United States.)

Meanwhile, a different battle raged on Minnesota soil, between the Dakota and the settlers. The U.S. government rarely kept its treaty promises, and the Dakota got little in return for lands they had sold. As their lands shrank, they grew hungrier and angrier. Then, on August 17, 1862,

Minnesota was a land of opportunity for early settlers like this farmer, shown in the field with his oxen-drawn plow.

Children were expected to help out with everyday tasks on the family farm.

a small band of Dakota attacked settlers near Acton. Three white men and two women died.

At first, Dakota chief Taoyateduta, or Little Crow, tried to keep peace. But other Dakota believed this was a good time to chase out the settlers, since so many men were off fighting in the Civil War. So Dakota warriors attacked farms and forts and burned buildings. Former governor Henry Sibley led a group of soldiers against the Dakota. By the time the Indians surrendered near the end of September, more than 400 settlers had been killed. The army rounded up 1,700 Dakota, including women, children, and elders as well as warriors. The warriors were put on trial and more than 300 were sentenced to death. President Abraham Lincoln reduced most of the sentences to prison terms, but he upheld the execution of thirty-eight Dakota. This was the biggest mass execution in U.S. history.

Quick Facts

HEAVY TRAFFIC
Logjams were common along the state's waterways. The worst was recorded in 1889. Logs backed up a 2.5-mile-long (4-km-long) stretch of the Saint Croix River; the pileup of logs was 100 feet (30 m) deep.

Loggers from the 1890s carry timber through the forest on a sled pulled by oxen.

Farmers, Loggers, and Miners

In the mid–1860s, Minnesota started a period of rapid growth. Land was cleared for farming in much of the southern, central, and western regions. The settlers suffered many hardships, including plagues of grasshoppers that destroyed their crops. But they worked hard to build a new life for themselves in this new land. By 1878, wheat, Minnesota's main crop, filled about 70 percent of the state's fields. This was good for the flour-milling industry in Minneapolis. In fact, the city had become known as the flour-milling capital of the world.

The logging industry started in central Minnesota in the mid–1800s. At first, American Indians were the region's main lumberjacks. They cut down trees and sent them downriver to lumber mills. As loggers cleared more land, they moved farther north. The logging industry in Minnesota reached its peak around 1900. Owners of lumber companies became rich. But they had cut down most of the state's white pines, and, in all, one-third of Minnesota's forests were gone.

Iron mines in Minnesota's Mesabi Range contributed to the state's economic development and population growth in the late 1800s and beyond.

In the late 1880s, a miner working for the Merritt family discovered a big deposit of iron in the Mesabi Range. Unlike other finds, this rich ore lay near the surface and was easy to reach. The first mine soon opened, and in time, Minnesota was supplying almost three-fourths of the nation's iron ore. Steel-making also became an important industry in the state. In 1916, U.S. Steel—one of the largest steel companies at the time—opened a steel mill near Duluth. It remained in operation for more than sixty years.

Workers Speak Out

Big companies took over many Minnesota industries, including mining, food processing, and manufacturing industries, as well as railroads. Factory workers often were paid low wages and struggled to make a decent living. But the first major call for change came from farmers. Besides the risk of bad weather and years of low prices for their crops, the farmers had to pay high rates to store their crops in giant towers called grain elevators. They also paid heavily to ship their crops to market by rail. They needed a way to reduce costs.

In 1867, a Minnesota farmer named Oliver H. Kelley began a group called the Grange to fight for the rights of the farmers. It spread rapidly throughout Minnesota and other farm states. Members bought equipment and supplies as a group in order to lower costs. They also elected people to government offices who

In Their Own Words

I long to see the great army of producers in our country, turn their eyes up from their work; . . . set them to thinking—let them feel that they are human beings, and the strength of the nation, their labor honorable, and farming the highest calling on earth.

—Oliver H. Kelley

would pass laws to help farmers. These laws, called the Grange Acts, limited the fees railroad and grain elevator owners could charge farmers. The Grange helped farmers throughout the country gain political and economic power.

Among other workers, iron miners banded together to seek, and sometimes go on strike for, better working conditions and pay. Walkouts also occurred among loggers and sawmill workers. Companies often responded by hiring men to break up the workers' organizations (labor unions) and force the workers to give up their protests.

Minnesota's most famous strike came when Minneapolis truckers walked off the job, calling for companies to recognize their union. The climax came on July 20, 1934, when police fired into a group of unarmed strikers. A few of the strikers died, and some two hundred were wounded. The day became known as Bloody Friday. The event helped build support for labor unions, not only in Minnesota but in the rest of the country as well.

Hard Times

By this time, the Great Depression was in full swing, and life was hard for workers throughout the country. In Minnesota, large numbers of factory workers and miners lost their jobs. Farmers were also affected by the hard times. Grain prices fell, and some farmers could not afford to plant new crops. In 1932, farmers called a strike to get higher prices for their crops. They blocked roads to prevent food from being delivered to big-city markets. A year later, they marched to the State Capitol in St. Paul. This time, they helped get a law passed to block banks from taking farms away from families who owed money and could not repay their loans.

World War II (in which the United States fought from 1941 to 1945) helped end the Depression in Minnesota and the rest of the nation. Farmers produced food for soldiers, and iron was needed for military equipment. Another milestone came in 1959, when the St. Lawrence Seaway opened. It allowed big ships from the Atlantic Ocean to sail all the way to Duluth at the western end of the Great Lakes, giving Minnesota's mines and other industries an international port.

Like many Minnesotans, this poor farm family, from Hollandale, suffered hardships during the Great Depression.

Modern Minnesota

Minnesotans have a strong tradition of thinking independently and speaking out to express their views. Minnesota's own political party, the Farmer-Labor Party, was the most powerful party in the state during the early 1900s. After it merged with the Democratic Party in 1944, the Democratic-Farmer-Labor Party (DFL) continued to produce influential political leaders, especially in the U.S. Senate. Minnesotans also showed their independence in 1998 when they elected Jesse "The Body" Ventura governor of Minnesota. Ventura was best known as a professional wrestler, sports commentator, and actor.

Along with the rest of the nation, Minnesota suffered from a recession, or downturn in the economy, that began at the end of 2007 and then became more severe. From mid–2008 to mid–2009, the state lost more than 100,000 jobs. However, the unemployment rate, or percentage of workers who were out of work and looking for a job, was still lower than the average for the United States as a whole.

Minnesota continues to be a place where people come first. As author and radio personality Garrison Keillor wrote, Minnesota "produces good-hearted people who are tolerant, helpful and friendly."

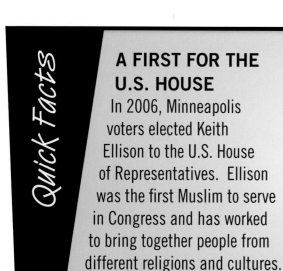

Quick Facts

A FIRST FOR THE U.S. HOUSE

In 2006, Minneapolis voters elected Keith Ellison to the U.S. House of Representatives. Ellison was the first Muslim to serve in Congress and has worked to bring together people from different religions and cultures.

★ **1660** French explorers Pierre Radisson and Médard Chouart, sieur des Groseilliers, travel through what is now southeastern Minnesota.

★ **1679** Daniel Greysolon, sieur Du Lhut, visits what is now Minnesota and helps strengthen French control over the region.

★ **1763** The British win the French and Indian War, and much of present-day Minnesota comes under British control.

★ **1783** With America's victory in the American Revolution, the part of Minnesota east of the Mississippi River becomes part of the United States.

★ **1803** The United States buys the Louisiana Territory from France, including the part of Minnesota west of the Mississippi River.

★ **1820** Colonel Josiah Snelling builds a U.S. fort in Minnesota near the Falls of Saint Anthony.

★ **1851** Most Dakota and Ojibwe are forced from their Minnesota land.

★ **1858** Minnesota becomes the thirty-second state.

★ **1862** The Dakota Conflict rages between settlers and the Dakota Indians.

★ **1867** Oliver H. Kelley establishes the farmers' group known as the Grange.

★ **1890** Iron ore is discovered in northeastern Minnesota.

★ **1959** The St. Lawrence Seaway is opened.

★ **1964** The Boundary Waters Canoe Area gains federal protection. Hubert Humphrey, a longtime U.S. senator from Minnesota, is elected vice president of the United States.

★ **1976** Senator Walter Mondale, another prominent Minnesotan, is elected U.S. vice president.

★ **1999** The U.S. Supreme Court upholds the rights of the Ojibwe to hunt and fish under their own rules.

★ **2007** A highway bridge across the Mississippi River in Minneapolis collapses, killing thirteen people.

★ **2009** Comedy writer Al Franken wins a legal battle to become a U.S. senator from Minnesota.

The People

Through the years, the hunt for land and jobs has brought waves of people to Minnesota. Today, Minnesota still attracts newcomers, both from other states and from foreign countries. Despite the long cold winters, the state ranks high in quality of life, with its excellent schools, lively midsize cities, quiet lakes, and welcoming neighbors. Minnesotans old and new belong to different races and ethnic groups, contributing their own customs, traditions, and holidays to life in the state.

According to U.S. Census Bureau estimates, Minnesota in 2007 had almost 5.2 million people, making it the twenty-first most populated state. As with other Midwestern states, the population has shifted in recent decades from country to city living. Almost three-fourths of Minnesotans now live in an urban area.

About 60 percent of the population lives in the

Quick Facts

URBAN HUB
Once referred to as the "Dual Cities," Minneapolis and St. Paul started out as small settlements and grew closer together as they expanded, until they formed one big urban area. The Twin Cities today serve as a cultural and business hub for the north-central United States. They draw visitors from all over the region and are home to many thriving businesses.

Two children read with their mentor in an after-school program in St. Paul.

City parks offer families open space for exercise and fresh air.

Minneapolis–St. Paul metropolitan area, which includes these two "Twin Cities" and the many smaller cities and suburbs surrounding them. Minneapolis by itself is the largest city, with an estimated population of 382,605 in 2008. Right on its border, across the Mississippi, is the city of St. Paul, the state capital. It had a population of 279,590 in 2008. Rochester, to the south, is the third-largest city (population, 100,413), and Duluth, on Lake Superior, ranks fourth, with 84,284 people as of 2008. Rochester and Duluth are the centers of their own metropolitan areas. But Minnesota's fifth-largest city, Bloomington (population, 81,280), is close to the Twin Cities and part of the Minneapolis–St. Paul metropolitan area. In fact, most of Minnesota's twenty biggest cities are part of that metropolitan area.

Ethnic Diversity

The face of Minnesota has changed over the years. The earliest residents were American Indians. French-Canadian fur trappers and missionaries were the first Europeans to arrive. They were followed by people of English heritage. In the 1800s, large numbers of German, Swedish,

Quick Facts

DO I HAVE TO EAT IT?
One tradition that has survived among many of Minnesota's Scandinavian Americans is that of eating lutefisk in the winter months. This dish consists of dried whitefish soaked for a long time in lye. Not everyone finds it tasty, and it is the subject of many jokes. The town of Madison, Minnesota, calls itself the "lutefisk capital" of the United States.

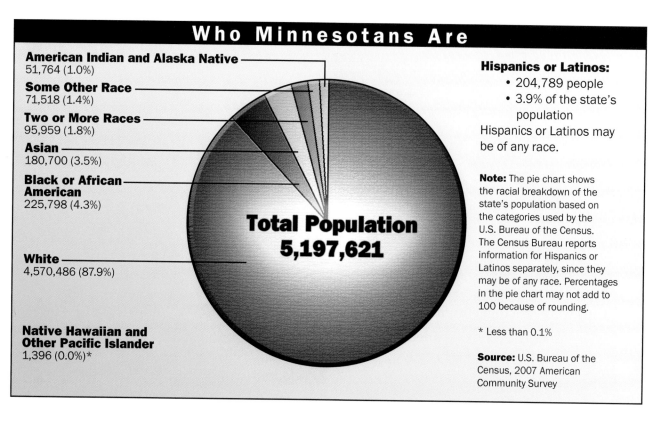

Who Minnesotans Are

American Indian and Alaska Native
51,764 (1.0%)

Some Other Race
71,518 (1.4%)

Two or More Races
95,959 (1.8%)

Asian
180,700 (3.5%)

Black or African American
225,798 (4.3%)

White
4,570,486 (87.9%)

Native Hawaiian and Other Pacific Islander
1,396 (0.0%)*

Total Population 5,197,621

Hispanics or Latinos:
- 204,789 people
- 3.9% of the state's population

Hispanics or Latinos may be of any race.

Note: The pie chart shows the racial breakdown of the state's population based on the categories used by the U.S. Bureau of the Census. The Census Bureau reports information for Hispanics or Latinos separately, since they may be of any race. Percentages in the pie chart may not add to 100 because of rounding.

* Less than 0.1%

Source: U.S. Bureau of the Census, 2007 American Community Survey

Norwegian, Danish, and Irish people settled in different parts of the state. The late 1800s also saw new waves of immigrants from Eastern Europe, including Polish and Czech people, and from Finland.

At first, members of these different ethnic groups spoke their own languages and kept to their old customs. Entire towns, such as New Ulm and Sleepy Eye, spoke German for decades. These groups still preserve elements of their cultural heritage. But over the years, they have become less distinct, blending in with the Midwestern lifestyle.

Today, most Minnesotans are of European background. But there are also African Americans, as well as Hispanic Americans who trace their ancestry to Latin America. Many recent immigrants to Minnesota are from parts of Asia and Africa. These people continue to make the state culturally diverse.

Many immigrants came from Southeast Asia after the end of the Vietnam War in 1975. People from groups that had aided the American side feared that

A German band performs at an ethnic festival in the town of New Ulm, where many German Americans keep old traditions alive.

they were in danger from Communist governments that had gained control of the region. Among these immigrants were Hmong people from the mountains of Vietnam or Laos. Minnesota today has more Hmong people than any other state except California.

Living in Minnesota was a big change, but the Hmong and others from Southeast Asia are making progress in adjusting to their new lives. In 2002, Mee Moua was elected to the Minnesota state senate, becoming the first-ever Hmong-American state legislator.

These boys playing ball in a Minnesota town are among many Hmong children who live in the state today.

Indians from a Minnesota reservation harvest wild rice, following a long tradition. They are using wooden sticks to knock the ripe rice grains into their boat.

Minnesota also has the largest Tibetan community in the United States outside New York, and the state has attracted many immigrants from African countries. The biggest group is from Somalia. War and poverty there have forced tens of thousands to leave their homeland. Church groups and others in Minnesota have helped immigrants resettle, and the state has developed programs to meet the special needs of immigrants and of minorities.

Most of the recent immigrants and members of minority groups in Minnesota, including African Americans and Hispanic Americans, have their largest communities in the Twin Cities. Parts of Minneapolis and St. Paul have an international flavor, with ethnic grocery stores and restaurants.

Adding to Minnesota's ethnic diversity are the more than 50,000 Ojibwe, Dakota, and other American Indian residents. Many Indians live in the Twin Cities. Some of the others live on reservations.

Sinclair Lewis: Writer

Sinclair Lewis was born in 1885 in Sauk Centre and grew up in that small Minnesota town. Eventually, he became a writer and lived in many different places. In *Main Street* (1920) and other widely read novels, he paints a picture of small-town life in America. In 1930, Lewis became the first American to win the Nobel Prize in Literature. He died in 1951.

Roy Wilkins: Journalist and Civil Rights Leader

Born in Missouri in 1901, Roy Wilkins grew up in St. Paul. He became a newspaper editor and a leader in the civil rights movement. He headed the National Association for the Advancement of Colored People (NAACP) for many years and worked for laws guaranteeing equal rights to African Americans. In 1969, Wilkins received the Presidential Medal of Freedom. He died in 1981. There is a memorial to him on the mall of the State Capitol in St. Paul.

Charles Schulz: Cartoonist

Everyone knows Snoopy. The famous cartoon dog, along with his owner, Charlie Brown, are among the familiar characters drawn by Charles Schulz. Born in Minneapolis in 1922, Schulz drew a weekly cartoon for a St. Paul newspaper before creating the famous comic strip *Peanuts*. His *Peanuts* characters have been known and loved around the world for sixty years. Schulz died in 2000.

Bob Dylan: Singer, Songwriter

Bob Dylan was born in Duluth in 1941 and grew up in Minnesota. During the 1960s and 1970s, his folk and rock music, with its messages calling for peace and equal rights, attracted millions of fans. In 1988, Dylan was inducted into the Rock and Roll Hall of Fame. He has received many other awards and honors.

Louise Erdrich: Writer

Louise Erdrich was born in 1954 in Little Falls, Minnesota, and grew up in North Dakota. As a child she learned about Ojibwe traditions from her grandfather, who had been the leader of a branch of the Ojibwe. She also gained a love of storytelling. Erdrich has written more than two dozen books, including some for children, and has earned many awards.

Briana Scurry: Athlete

Briana Scurry is an American soccer star who broke barriers for African Americans in the sport. Born in Minneapolis in 1971, she grew up in Minnesota and went to the University of Massachusetts on an athletic scholarship. There she starred as a goalie. During the 1990s and the early 2000s, Scurry helped the U.S. National Team gain both World Cup and Olympic victories. She has since played on several professional soccer teams.

A teacher works with students in a classroom in St. Paul.

Good Schools for Everyone

Surveys have ranked Minnesota near the top among U.S. states in providing high-quality public schools. The state also ranks near the top for the percentage of residents who have graduated from high school.

School officials and teachers have often been leaders in finding new ways to improve education. For example, in 1992 the nation's first charter school opened in the state of Minnesota. Charter schools are free public schools that are run separately from the public school system. They try new or different teaching methods and were created to help more students do well in school. Today, the state has about 150 charter schools with about 30,000 pupils.

In addition, schools often have special programs devoted to the culture of particular ethnic groups, and many schools, especially in urban areas, provide classes in Spanish or certain African, Asian, or American Indian languages to help meet the needs of students.

On the college level, the University of Minnesota, with campuses in the Twin Cities and four other locations, has one of the best reputations of any state university. The state also has a fine system of state colleges and many excellent private colleges, including Carleton College and St. Olaf College, in Northfield, and Macalester College in St. Paul, to name a few.

In Their Own Words

Welcome to Lake Wobegon, where all the men are strong, all the women are good-looking, and all the children are above average.

—Author and Minnesota native Garrison Keillor, introducing the made-up Minnesota town of Lake Wobegon on his popular radio show.

One of the largest and most respected university systems in the nation, the University of Minnesota serves more than 60,000 students and offers some 370 degree programs. Shown here is a portion of the main campus in Minneapolis.

★ Icebox Days

Every January, the people of International Falls celebrate the winter season. Residents and visitors can enjoy candlelight skiing, an old-fashioned bonfire, ice skating, snowshoe races, snow and ice sculptures, and the "freeze yer gizzard" blizzard run.

★ Burns Night

On a chilly January night in 1876, Scottish farmers in Mapleton read Robert Burns's poetry to remember their homeland. Each year, the town continues the tradition with a poetry reading, Scottish songs and food, and bagpipe music.

★ St. Paul Winter Carnival

In January, this city hosts the country's oldest and largest winter festival. Highlights include cultural celebrations, parades, contests, snow sculpting, a snow slide, and an ice palace.

★ Festival of Nations

Since 1932, St. Paul has hosted one of the nation's largest and oldest celebrations of international culture. The event, which is held in the spring, offers dance, food, and art from various countries.

★ Lefse Dagen (Pancake Day)

In 1983, people from the town of Starbuck built a 10-foot-by-10-foot (3-m-by-3-m) griddle. Eight bakers prepared dough made from 32 pounds (14.5 kg) of potatoes, 30 pounds (13.6 kg) of flour, 2 pounds (0.9 kg) of sugar, and 4 pounds (1.8 kg) of shortening. Then they baked the biggest *lefse* (potato pancake) on record, for the whole town to eat. Each May, Starbuck celebrates this event.

★ Land of the Loon Festival

In June, hundreds of Minnesotans gather in the city of Virginia to honor the state bird. Activities include a parade, arts-and-crafts displays, food, music, and magic acts.

★ Bavarian Blast

The entire town of New Ulm comes alive with an old-world German festival in July. Singers trill, tubas oompah, and crowds enjoy German foods, crafts, and costumes.

★ Lumberjack Days

In honor of the state's lumber history, Stillwater, in July, holds a parade, treasure hunt, and contests for log rolling, chainsaw carving, ax throwing, and speed pole climbing.

★ White Oak Rendezvous

Rendezvous is a French word for "meeting." Every year, during the first weekend in August, visitors dressed as French fur traders come together to camp at White Oak Fur Post, near Deer Creek. They share meals, sleep under the stars, and join in shooting, music, dancing, and singing.

★ *Wacipi*

Wacipi, which means "dance" in Dakota, is an important part of the powwow held each year in Mankato in September. This event is one of several held there at which Indians celebrate their rich culture.

★ Minnesota State Fair

Every year in late August and early September, St. Paul holds a state fair that brings the farms to the big city. Agricultural exhibits, animal shows, and baking contests share the stage with musical acts and industrial displays. The dairy industry has a contest to select a young woman as its "princess," and statues of the finalists are displayed at the fair, each carved out of butter. There is also plenty of food on hand. The fair attracted almost 2 million people in 2009.

How the Government Works

Many government workers serve Minnesota by helping to run the state's cities, townships, and counties. These are all different units of local government.

Four out of five Minnesotans live in cities, although these cities take up only about 5 percent of the state's land area. Most of Minnesota's more than eight hundred cities are small, with between one thousand and ten thousand people. About a hundred are "charter cities." This means that they can decide, within limits, the type of local government that fits their needs and then write their own charter, or set of rules. The rest of the cities are called statutory cities. They follow the laws and guidelines that the state has adopted for local governments. Most Minnesota cities are governed by an elected city council and elected mayor. But in some cities, a city manager is hired by the elected council.

The state also has close to 1,800 townships. Many townships cover large rural areas that have small populations. Each township is governed by an elected board of supervisors that usually has three members. In townships, many important decisions are made by citizens themselves at an annual town meeting.

On a higher level, the state is divided into eighty-seven counties. A five- or seven-member board of commissioners manages each county. Voters elect board members to four-year terms. They also might elect a county attorney, recorder, sheriff, treasurer, and auditor for four-year terms. Along with the

The State Capitol in St. Paul is a center of government and a Minnesota landmark.

Branches of Government

EXECUTIVE ★ ★ ★ ★ ★ ★ ★ ★

The executive branch is headed by the governor, who is elected to a four-year term. The lieutenant governor, secretary of state, auditor, and attorney general are also elected to four-year terms. The governor supervises the state government, plans the budget, and appoints other officials to help carry out the state's programs.

LEGISLATIVE ★ ★ ★ ★ ★ ★ ★ ★

The legislative branch makes the state's laws. It has two chambers, or parts: the senate and the house of representatives. The senate has 67 members, elected for four-year terms (or for two-year terms in years ending in 0). The house has 134 members, elected for two-year terms.

JUDICIAL ★ ★ ★ ★ ★ ★ ★ ★

The judicial branch applies the state's laws in court cases and sometimes decides whether a law is allowed under the state constitution. At the lowest level, there about three hundred district courts, hearing some 2 million cases a year. Their rulings can be appealed to one of the nineteen appellate courts and then to the state supreme court. The supreme court, the state's highest court, has six associate justices and one chief justice. In Minnesota, all judges are elected. They serve six-year terms.

cities and townships, the counties provide a variety of important services to people in Minnesota.

State and Federal Government

The state government, like the federal (national) government, is divided into three branches: executive, legislative, and judicial. The center of Minnesota's state government is the capital, St. Paul.

Minnesotans elect lawmakers to represent them in the U.S. Congress in Washington, D.C. Like all other states, Minnesota has two U.S. senators. The number of members a state sends to the U.S. House of Representatives is based on its population. As of 2010, Minnesota had eight representatives in the House.

How a Bill Becomes a Law

A bill is a proposed law or change in a law. Only someone from the legislative branch of government can start a bill on the process required for it to become state law.

Members of the Minnesota house of representatives meet here to debate and vote on the state's laws.

The bill must first be presented, or introduced, by a senator or representative. From there, it goes to a committee of the senate or house, wherever the bill's sponsor serves. After discussing the bill, committee members reject or approve it.

If the committee approves the bill, members of the whole chamber study and discuss it. Sometimes, they may change parts of the bill or add or remove parts of it. If the bill passes in the chamber where it was first proposed, it moves to the other chamber. Both chambers must pass the exact same bill before it can go to the governor. If the second chamber approves the bill but makes changes in it, the bill goes to a special committee in which members from both the house of representatives and the senate work to resolve the differences.

Once both chambers have passed the exact same bill by a majority vote, it goes to the governor. The governor can sign the bill, in which case it becomes law. The governor can also allow a bill to become law by taking no action on it. If the governor disagrees with the bill, he or she can veto, or reject, it. If the governor vetoes the bill, it goes back to the legislature, where it can be voted on again. It can still become law—but only if it is again passed by a two-thirds vote in both the house and the senate.

Minnesota's state legislators have made new laws in many different areas, from energy and the environment to traffic, crime, education, and taxes. Many recent state laws are meant to help consumers and safeguard people's safety and health. For example, the legislature recently passed a law to ban the sale of unsafe toys. Another new measure protects consumers from having to pay for calls made when their cell phone is stolen. And another law set up a group to study how the state can help people with Alzheimer's disease.

A Voice in Government

"Our government was founded on the idea that anyone can make a difference," writes a Minnesota government official. "If you think [that] issues won't be of interest until you're older, think again." Minnesotans must be eighteen years old to vote. But that does not mean that younger people cannot have a say in

FROM FOOTBALL FIELD TO SUPREME COURT

Alan Page was a star football player at Notre Dame University and then for fifteen years in the National Football League, playing for the Minnesota Vikings and Chicago Bears. He earned his law degree from the University of Minnesota, going to law school full time while playing pro football. In 1992, Page was elected to serve on the Minnesota supreme court. He often speaks to students in Minnesota schools about the value of education.

Alan Page was elected an associate justice of the state supreme court in 1992.

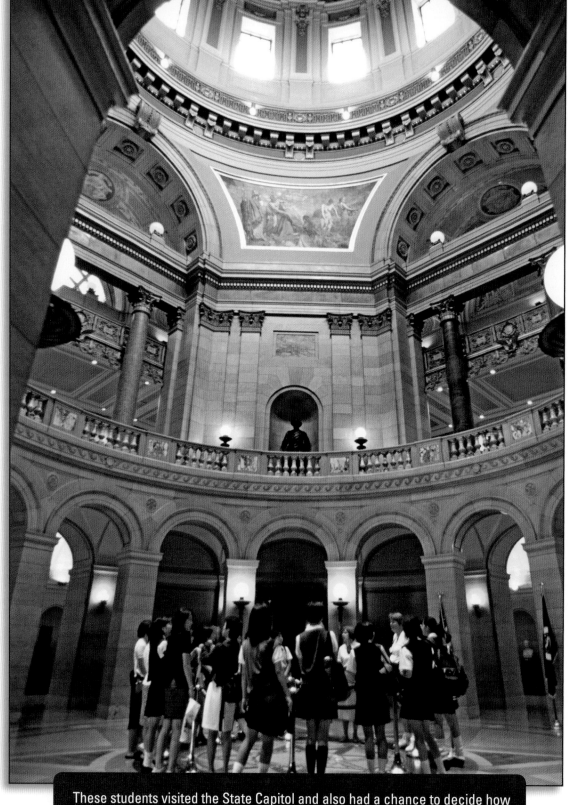

These students visited the State Capitol and also had a chance to decide how they would vote on twelve different issues facing the state government.

what happens in their state and nation. Young Minnesotans find many ways to participate in government.

Project Citizen has civics programs for students in grades five to twelve. One program encourages students to work together to define a public problem. Then they think of ways to solve it and develop a plan to put their ideas to work. After writing the plan, students can send their report to be judged by legislators and community leaders. A number of middle-school students in Minnesota have participated in Project Citizen. One group recently worked on the issue of smoking in public. As part of the project, they followed the progress of the "Freedom to Breathe" bill as it made its way through the state legislature. This measure, which became a law and went into effect in 2007, banned smoking indoors in public places.

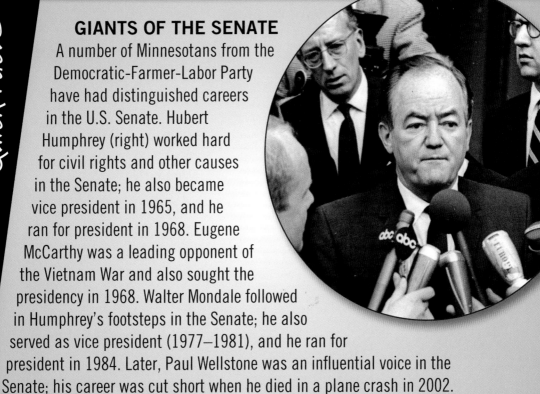

Quick Facts

GIANTS OF THE SENATE

A number of Minnesotans from the Democratic-Farmer-Labor Party have had distinguished careers in the U.S. Senate. Hubert Humphrey (right) worked hard for civil rights and other causes in the Senate; he also became vice president in 1965, and he ran for president in 1968. Eugene McCarthy was a leading opponent of the Vietnam War and also sought the presidency in 1968. Walter Mondale followed in Humphrey's footsteps in the Senate; he also served as vice president (1977–1981), and he ran for president in 1984. Later, Paul Wellstone was an influential voice in the Senate; his career was cut short when he died in a plane crash in 2002.

Making a Living

Minnesota began as a farm state, and agriculture remains an important part of the economy, though farming itself does not account for many jobs. Minnesota's forests and mines are other important resources. Many businesses in Minnesota turn the state's crops and other natural resources and raw materials into goods that are then sold nationwide. One example is General Mills, based in Golden Valley, which makes more than a hundred brands of food products, from Hamburger Helper to Cheerios.

Minnesota universities and businesses join together to create new products and improve old ones. Some common household items, including see-through adhesive tape and Post-it® notes, were invented in Minnesota. Retail stores employ many thousands of people in Minnesota. The largest shopping mall in the United States, the Mall of America, is located in Bloomington. But not all Minnesota jobs involve creating and selling goods. Many of the state's largest industries, including health care, education, and tourism, are service industries.

Farming in Minnesota

Minnesota is a major farm state. It is among the top four states for growing feed corn and soybeans—the state's most valuable crops. Minnesota is also a leading producer of wheat, oats, barley, potatoes, dried beans, and several seeds used in cooking oils and biodiesel fuels. Year after year, it is the number one

Farming is still vital to Minnesota's economy
and a livelihood for farm families like this one.

Minnesota is a top state in growing corn, peas, and other vegetables for freezing or canning.

grower of sugar beets, as well as of corn and peas for freezing or canning. Minnesota is also a key dairy state, and it is among the main states for raising and marketing pigs and for producing red meat. Finally, Minnesota raises more turkeys than any other state.

Minnesota vies with California as the nation's largest producer of cultivated wild rice. But California has no native beds of wild rice. In Minnesota, on the other hand, truly wild rice thrives in numerous lakes and marshes in large areas of the state. American Indians continue to gather wild rice using traditional methods that are centuries old.

Farmers in Minnesota have had a long tradition of working together to grow and sell what they produce. To do this, they formed organizations called cooperatives, which help farmers reduce their costs and also can reduce prices for consumers. The idea of cooperatives can be traced back to Minnesota's Scandinavian immigrants. Today, there are hundreds of cooperatives in operation in the state, including grain elevators, energy suppliers, dairies, and many other kinds. Some of the state's most successful international businesses are still cooperatives.

Minnesota Manufacturing

Making crops into food products is a leading business in Minnesota, and the state is home to some of the world's biggest food-processing companies. For

Workers & Industries

Industry	Number of People Working in That Industry	Percentage of All Workers Who Are Working in That Industry
Education and health care	621,878	23%
Wholesale and retail businesses	402,152	15%
Manufacturing	391,209	14%
Publishing, media, entertainment, hotels, and restaurants	285,349	10%
Professionals, scientists, and managers	252,340	9%
Banking and finance, insurance, and real estate	207,253	8%
Construction	186,827	7%
Transportation and public utilities	125,378	5%
Other services	122,101	4%
Government	88,348	3%
Farming, fishing, forestry, and mining	65,187	2%
Totals	2,748,022	100%

Notes: Figures above do not include people in the armed forces. "Professionals" includes people such as doctors and lawyers. Percentages may not add to 100 because of rounding.

Source: U.S. Bureau of the Census, 2007 estimates

One of the state's best-known food products is the canned meat called SPAM®. Introduced by Minnesota-based Hormel Foods in the 1930s, it can be found today on grocery shelves in some forty countries around the world.

example, General Mills started in the 1860s as a flour mill on the Mississippi River. Land O' Lakes started in the 1920s as a cooperative to sell butter. Hormel Foods began as a meatpacking company in the 1890s and in the 1930s became famous for its canned meats. Today, these companies sell their original products, as well as hundreds of other packaged foods, throughout the world.

Minnesota's forests are important in the state's industries. Loggers manage the forests, harvesting trees for manufacturing paper and paper products, as well as for furniture and construction materials. In recent years, Minnesota has ranked first among all the states in the manufacture of wooden doors and windows.

RECIPE FOR WILD RICE SOUP

The Ojibwe and Dakota have been gathering wild rice in Minnesota for hundreds of years. This soup, featuring wild rice, is delicious for lunch or for dinner.

WHAT YOU NEED

1 box seasoned wild rice

2 tablespoons (20 g) onion, cut into very small pieces

1 cup (150 g) celery, chopped fine

4 tablespoons (60 grams) butter

$\frac{1}{2}$ cup (60 g) all-purpose flour

6 cups (1.5 liters) chicken or vegetable broth

1 teaspoon (5 g) dried parsley

Salt and pepper, according to your taste

$1\frac{1}{2}$ cups (350 milliliters) cream

Chives, cut into very small pieces

Cook the wild rice according to the instructions on the package. You can prepare the other ingredients while the rice is cooking.

Ask an adult to help you chop the onion and celery. Melt the butter in a soup pot and add the onion and celery. Have an adult help you cook this mixture until the pieces are soft. Add the flour and cook for two minutes more, stirring often.

Next add the broth and parsley, along with salt and pepper. As it cooks, stir the mixture constantly until it becomes thicker. Add the cooked rice and then the cream. Heat well, but be careful not to bring the soup to a boil. Spoon into bowls and sprinkle some chives on top. When it is cool enough to eat, dig in and enjoy!

Minnesota is also a leader in manufacturing many kinds of high-tech equipment. Factories turn out everything from supercomputers and computer software to the latest medical devices and supplies. Important health-care breakthroughs include blood pumps, pacemakers for damaged hearts, and hearing aids.

This statue in Bemidji, of Paul Bunyan with his blue ox, Babe, reminds us that Minnesota has a long tradition as a logging state.

THE LEGEND OF PAUL BUNYAN

Minnesotans love Paul Bunyan—the legendary wood-cutting giant—and his ox, Babe. According to one story, Bunyan cleared an entire forest with a single sweep of his ax. There are huge statues of Paul Bunyan in Brainerd, Bemidji, and Akeley. These and other Minnesota towns also claim to have things that belonged to him. As you travel around the state, you may come across Paul Bunyan's dog, pet squirrel, ax, harmonica, mailbox, and even his footprint.

This statue of an ironworker, in Chisholm, stands 36 feet (11 m) tall and testifies to the importance of the industry for Minnesota. The state is still a leading iron producer.

Mining in Minnesota

Mining has been an important industry in Minnesota for more than a hundred years. At one time, high-grade iron ore accounted for most of the mining industry. By the 1950s, however, most of this ore had been mined. Mining companies then turned their attention to a low-grade ore called taconite. They developed new methods to extract iron from taconite. To this day, Minnesota remains the nation's main supplier of iron ore. In recent years, Minnesota has also been the nation's leading producer of cut stone. Quarries in different parts of the state mine granite, limestone, sandstone, and other kinds of stone used as building materials.

Quick Facts

THE FIRST RIDERS WERE MINERS

In 1914, Swedish immigrant Carl Wickman started a bus service that brought iron miners from Hibbing to Alice. That was the beginning of the Greyhound Bus Company. Today, Greyhound buses carry some 25 million passengers a year to thousands of towns and cities in the United States, Canada, Mexico, and Great Britain.

Corn

Southern Minnesota sits in the Midwestern corn belt. This is where farms grow large amounts of corn. Most of Minnesota's corn is used to feed beef cattle, but some is canned or frozen and shipped to grocery stores around the world.

Computers and Electronics

Minnesota is a leader in producing and developing electronic equipment. Computers, medical instruments, telephones, and many other items are made in Minnesota factories and shipped around the world.

Flour

The state grows less wheat than in the past. But it is still a key state in turning wheat into flour. Minnesota companies make the flour into foods, such as breakfast cereals, cake mixes, and baked goods.

Dairy Farms

With almost 500,000 dairy cattle, Minnesota is a top milk supplier. With its productive dairy farms, the state is also a leading manufacturer of dairy goods, including butter and cheese.

Pulp and Paper

Minnesota's forests provide timber for scrap board and paper products. Large paper mills can be found in such places as International Falls, Grand Rapids, Sartell, Cloquet, and Duluth.

Iron

Large deposits of iron ore still lie in the Mesabi Range. Once the ore is mined, it is sent by truck or by train to a processing plant. There, the ore is ground into a fine powder, the iron is extracted by a magnet, and the iron powder is formed into marble-size pellets. The pellets are usually shipped from Duluth to steel mills along the Great Lakes or elsewhere around the world.

Services, Sales, and Tourism

The largest number of Minnesotans work in service industries, such as hospitals, schools, insurance agencies, utility companies, transportation and shipping firms, banks and other financial institutions, government agencies, hotels, restaurants, and stores of all kinds.

Wholesale and retail sales are important to Minnesota's economy. For example, some 12,000 people work at the Mall of America. With more than 500 stores, 50 restaurants, and an indoor amusement park, the mall is the largest

Complete with its own indoor amusement park, the Mall of America, in Bloomington, is the nation's biggest shopping mall. Retail sales are a vital part of the state's economy.

Ice fishing is just one of the attractions that lure Minnesotans outdoors in winter and draw in hardy visitors from other states.

in the country. Besides selling products, the mall is part of Minnesota's tourist industry. It attracts around 40 million visitors every year—more than the Grand Canyon, Walt Disney World, and Elvis Presley's home, Graceland, combined.

Another important tourist attraction is the outdoors. Minnesotans and visitors alike enjoy the state's waters, woods, and fields. More than a million fishing licenses are sold every year, and there is one boat for every six people in the state. In fact, water skis were invented by a Minnesotan. Fans of winter sports love to skate, ski, snowboard, or ride across the winter landscape in snowmobiles. The first snowmobile was invented in Minnesota, as well. The state's government has made efforts to regulate tourism so as to preserve the environment while still allowing Minnesotans the opportunity to fully enjoy the state's natural beauty and many opportunities for recreation. One example of regulation is the rule that allows only nonmotorized boats in the Boundary Waters Canoe Area Wilderness.

Quick Facts

SMALL BEGINNINGS

In the late 1800s, Rochester doctors Will and Charlie Mayo and their father, William, discovered new ways to treat people who were ill. They formed a group of doctors who worked together, and it grew into the world-famous Mayo Clinic. Today, every year more than 300,000 patients come to Minnesota's Mayo Clinic for advice or treatment. The clinic also has branches in Arizona and Florida.

Besides participating in outdoor sports, visitors and residents like to root for the state's professional sports teams. Minnesota's Major League Baseball team is the Twins, named after the Twin Cities. Fans cheer on the Minnesota Vikings during the National Football League season. The Lynx are the Women's National Basketball Association team, while the men's National Basketball Association team is the Timberwolves.

In the year 2000, seven years after the Minnesota North Stars moved away, the state again got a National Hockey League team of its own, the Wild. There are also hundreds of recreational and school hockey teams in Minnesota. With their love of winter sports and their huge supply of winter ice and snow, it is no wonder that Minnesotans have named ice hockey the official state sport.

Minnesota's flag is royal blue with a seal (almost identical to the state seal) in the center. A wreath appears around the seal. The wreath displays the state flower along with three years: 1819 (the year Fort Snelling was established), 1858 (the year of statehood), and 1893 (the year the first flag was adopted). Because Minnesota was the nineteenth state admitted after the original thirteen states, nineteen stars are on the flag.

The state seal shows a farmer in a field of grain near the Mississippi River and an American Indian on horseback. The state motto, "Star of the North," appears in French over the scene.

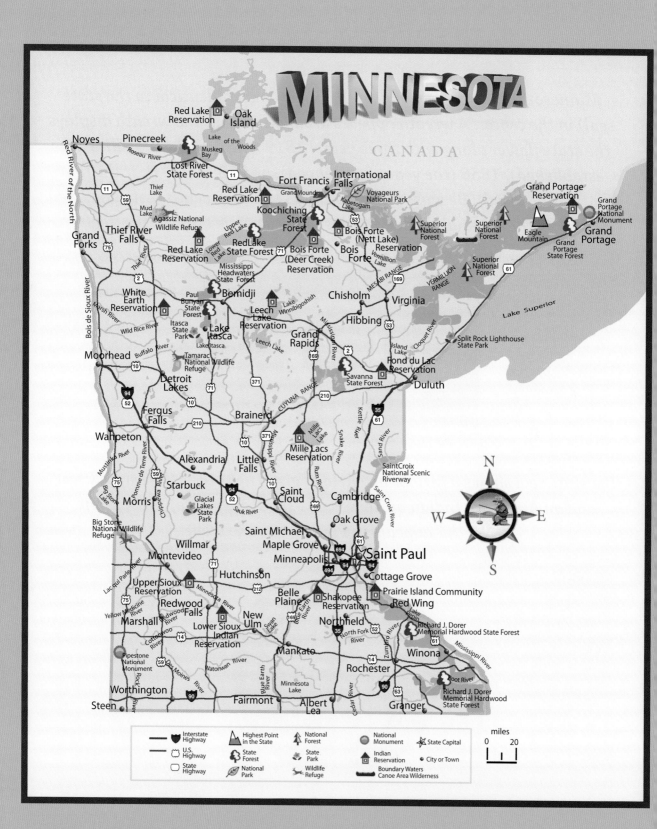

MINNESOTA

CANADA

Noyes • Pinecreek • Oak Island
Red Lake Reservation
Lake of the Woods
Muskeg Bay
Roseau River

Lost River State Forest

Thief Lake
11
59
Mud Lake
Thief River Falls

Agassiz National Wildlife Refuge

Red Lake Reservation
Fort Francis
Grand Mound
International Falls
Voyageurs National Park
Kabetogam Lake

Koochiching State Forest

53

Superior National Forest

Grand Portage Reservation
Grand Portage National Monument

Grand Forks
75

Upper Red Lake

Red Lake State Forest
71

Bois Forte (Nett Lake) Reservation
Bois Forte

Superior National Forest

Eagle Mountain
Grand Portage State Forest
Grand Portage

White Earth Reservation

Red Lake Reservation
Lower Red Lake

Bois Forte (Deer Creek) Reservation

Vermillion Lake

Superior National Forest
61

Moorhead
10

Bois de Sioux River
Marsh River

Wild Rice River

Buffalo River

Paul Bunyan State Forest
Mississippi Headwaters State Forest
Bemidji

Itasca State Park
Lake Itasca

Lake Winnibigoshish

Leech Lake Reservation

Leech Lake

Chisholm • Virginia
Hibbing
53

MESABI RANGE
169

VERMILLION RANGE
Lake Superior

Tamarac National Wildlife Refuge

Grand Rapids
169

Mississippi River

2

Island Lake
Cloquet River

Split Rock Lighthouse State Park

Detroit Lakes
10

Fergus Falls
94
52
210

Brainerd
371
210

CUYUNA RANGE

Fond du Lac Reservation
Savanna State Forest
Duluth

Wahpeton

Mustinka River

Alexandria
Little Falls
371
10

Mille Lacs Lake
Mille Lacs Reservation

Snake River
Kettle River
35
61

Saint Croix National Scenic Riverway

Starbuck
94
52

Glacial Lakes State Park

Saint Cloud
169

Cambridge

Saint Croix River

Morris

Pomme de Terre River
Chippewa River
Sauk River

Rum River

Big Stone Lake
59
75

Big Stone National Wildlife Refuge

Willmar
Montevideo
71

Hutchinson

Saint Michael
Maple Grove
Minneapolis
694
494
213

Oak Grove
61

Saint Paul
94
35
494

N
W   E
S

Cottage Grove

Upper Sioux Reservation

Lac qui Parle River
Minnesota River

Shakopee Reservation
Belle Plaine

Prairie Island Community
Red Wing

Redwood Falls

Yellow Medicine River
Redwood River

New Ulm

Blue Earth River
Swan Lake
169

Northfield
52

Lake Pepin

Richard J. Dorer Memorial Hardwood State Forest

Marshall

Cottonwood River
14

Lower Sioux Indian Reservation

35
North Fork River

Zumbro River
61

Winona
Mississippi River

Pipestone National Monument
59

Mankato

Des Moines River
Watonwan River

Blue Earth River

Cedar River

Minnesota Lake

Rochester
90
63

Root River

Richard J. Dorer Memorial Hardwood State Forest

Worthington
90

Steen

Fairmont

Albert Lea

Granger

miles
0   20

Interstate Highway	Highest Point in the State	National Forest	National Monument	State Capital
U.S. Highway	State Forest	State Park	Indian Reservation	City or Town
State Highway	National Park	Wildlife Refuge	Boundary Waters Canoe Area Wilderness	

Hail! Minnesota

words by Truman Elwell Rickard and
Arthur Wheelock Upson
music by Truman Elwell Rickard

BOOKS

Heinrichs, Ann. *Minnesota*. Chanhassen, MN: Child's World, 2006.

Johnson, Robin. *The Mississippi: America's Mighty River*. New York: Crabtree Publishing, 2010.

LeBoutillier, Nate. *The Story of the Minnesota Twins*. Mankato, MN: Creative Education, 2008.

Palazzo-Craig, Janet. *The Ojibwe of Michigan, Wisconsin, Minnesota, and North Dakota*. New York: PowerKids Press, 2005.

Schwabacher, Martin, and Patricia K. Kummer. *Minnesota*. New York: Benchmark Books, 2008.

Stewart, Mark. *The Minnesota Timberwolves*. Chicago: Norwood Press, 2009.

Vogel, Jennifer. *A Library Story: Building a New Central Library*. Minneapolis: Millbrook Press, 2007.

WEBSITES

Minnesota Department of Natural Resources:
http://www.dnr.state.mn.us

Minnesota Department of Tourism:
http://www.exploreminnesota.com

State of Minnesota Official Website:
http://www.state.mn.us

Marlene Targ Brill writes about many topics, from history and biographies to sports, world peace, and health issues. Each of her more than fifty books takes her on another journey, where she sees exciting places and meets interesting people. Minnesota is one of those places. Before launching her writing career, she taught students with special needs and teachers learning to work with them. She and her family live in Illinois.

Elizabeth Kaplan has edited textbooks and reference works on a wide variety of subjects. She has also written several science and social studies books for young adults. Throughout her life, she has enjoyed going on road trips. In her travels, she has been to forty-seven of the fifty states, including Minnesota. She lives in Wisconsin with her husband and two daughters.

Page numbers in **boldface** are illustrations.